MYSTIC WINES

POEMS

BY

JOHN LARS ZWERENZ

ISBN 13: 978-1722957438

Published by ATLApublishing.com

Art work by Sian Defferary©

MYSTIC WINES

1 THE REGAL DAWN

2 ODE TO BRAM STOKER

3 THE GARDEN

4 DUSK

5 THE SONG OF JOHN KEATS

6 THE GROVE

7 THE GHOST SHIP

8 DIADEMS

9 THE LANE

10 THE SHRINE OF SAINT ANNE

11 THE WINDOW BAY

12 STILLED BY A SIGH

A WORD FROM THE AUTHOR

Mystic Wines is my tenth and latest book of poetry, consisting of 40 all new poems. This work was begun with the hope that it would be written and completed according to the inspirations of The Holy Spirit, to the Good Will of God, in keeping with His providential wisdom. Now that Mystic Wines is completed, I hope and indeed believe that this aspiration was achieved, at least to a significant extent, and that the other, more incidental aspirations of this new collection were realized and brought to a successful conclusion. My vocation of being called to write poetry, to being a poet was always pursued and lived with a spirit of self sacrifice and in service to God and to my neighbors. In this art form there was never any room for furthering my own name, to seek fame or renown, or to pursue money for money's sake nor to display talents as if they belonged to myself, when in fact they are gifts from God. I wish to thank my publisher for all of the

II

kindness she has shown to me during the creative process of this anthology and to the litany of friends, teachers and family members who have supported me throughout the years in my service to the public as a poet. I am forever indebted to these wonderful people, and indeed to many more.

JOHN LARS ZWERENZ, NEW YORK, 2018

INTRODUCTION TO MYSTIC WINES

At some point while one is reading a book, be it a novel, a play, or a collection of poems, the reader goes back to the Introduction in the hopes of understanding the writer better. True, he may wait until he is finished or he might stop in the middle of a page and return to the Introduction to find out "Who is the writer? And what does he want to say?" If that happens with this volume of poetry by John Zwerenz, the writer of this introduction can answer: "I know him. He is my former student and my friend."

III

I met John Zwerenz in September of 1986 when he entered my humanities class in that golden year when he was a senior in high school. A colleague had recommended him saying, "I am sending you an amazing student. I placed that amazing student in the last seat of the last row only because his name began with a Z, but I saw right away that he was listening intently. Here was that rara avis in a classroom, a genuine learner.

It is an axiom that the poetic flame burns brightest in youth. In youth Hope is at its apex. The "real world" has its way of stealing imagination's thunder and imposing its peculiar drabness over the poetic faculties. Not so with John. Life became a school with many classrooms and his humanities class broadened into Humanity's Classroom. Now, nearing fifty, the one time student poet who sat in that last seat is enjoying a final bloom of Autumn.

Long ago I remember him stopping by my desk to compliment me on my Sappho lecture. Soon after he began to share his fondness for French Symbolists like Verlaine and Baudelaire. He was also steeped in philosophy and theology.

But Poetry was his Mistress. It dominated his thoughts and his actions. One day he missed class

IV

because he had overslept on a bed of grass in the cemetery adjacent to the school, having fallen asleep while musing on death. Death troubled him; its strangeness perplexed him. His language teacher had just died in the middle of the semester and John said, "Last week he was here, this week he is not; it's as if he had never been here. A new teacher has taken his place, but where did Mr__ go?" Death was the nexus between poetry and philosophy.

As for philosophy, he was reading Nietzsche at the time and John was troubled by a priest's comment: "God forgives atheists, but never Nietzsche." I didn't have an answer.

Poetry consoled him, fired his emotions, consumed his energy. He always carried some book of poetry in the halls. Poetry books were like kindling wood. Beside poetry, math and science were banal.

One day after class he played the Tempter and asked me what I thought of some lines he had written. I read them and quipped,
"Pretentious."
"They were written by Rimbaud."
I didn't have an answer for this either.

Those were also the days of endless classes on The Iliad and The Inferno. They took notes dutifully
V
but John found note taking distracting. He was intent on absorbing the material by listening and storing it in his mind. When he raised his hand to ask a question or to answer one, his classmates accorded him the same respect they accorded me. Of himself at that time, John writes,

I was 17 years of age that spring, and from that day onward I immersed myself in just about any poet of renown that I could find. Aside from the French Symbolists of Rimbaud's era, such as Verlaine, Nerval and Baudelaire, I also fell in love with the great romantic bards from Victorian England and America such as Byron, Shelley, and especially our own Edgar Allan Poe. By the time I entered undergraduate school at Queens College in New York, I was thoroughly proficient in my own poetic knowledge. Not in just being able to recognize good or great poetry from inferior verse, but in composing great metered, rhyming poetry I started to bloom.

In what may be his final volume of verse, John the wanderer looks for a place to rest. By the end he has found one. He is the narrator in The Lane:

We walked as angels in the rosy breeze,
Among holly green hedgerows (just us two).
The lane was gold and the sky was blue,
                    VI
And we heard through the boughs rare symphonies,
As the grasses framed your naked knees.

He is a second Keats musing on art:

…humble poets seek to learn

Wisdom from the secrets of a Grecian urn
(The Song of John Keats,)

He is the figure on Keats' Grecian Urn, that *Fair
youth, beneath the trees, thou canst not leave Thy song...
Forever wilt thou love, and she be fair! ... happy
melodist, unwearied, Forever piping songs forever
new... Forever panting, and forever young.....*

His wandering has led him to his own back yard
where he rests from the Muse that has been
whispering to him:

The iridescent sky
At the peak of its beauty
Reigns like a cosmic oligarchy...infinite peace is
married to delight....
There are pianos playing in the trees by the piers
On either side of the breeze blown lane.
There are mystic wines within the rain,
Which sanctify my pages, wet - as with tears

There he has built a bower with statuary—not of
Greek gods and goddesses--but of the angels and
saints of Christendom, and especially to Mary, the
Mother of God. His poetry has turned devotional.
He is not inspired by French symbolists but by
French saints, like Therese of Lisieux and Louis de
Montfort. His garden is his "shrine upon a down." In
sanctity he finds his worthiest subject.

Beyond the maze of city streets,
Where sounds become suburban retreats
I found a shrine upon a down.

Silhouettes of oaks, and an iron fence
Found me amid blooms which marked the entrance.
....in one corner of the shrine's pure light
I beheld the spirit of good Saint Anne,
And discovered what it means to be a holy man.
                    (St Anne's Shrine)
....
....

As an English teacher, I was interested in his
poems on English writers like Stoker, Keats, Byron,
and Stevenson:

My love can not be found in the verse of Poe.
Nor in Shakespeare's litanies of the wise man's
woe.
Verily, I tell you, you will not find her there,
Resting upon a balcony, in a state of swooning,
mad despair.
No Romeo can lure her from my arms…
                    VIII
His Ode to Bram Stoker is worth quoting at length.
He loved the novel Dracula but ruthlessly critiques
Stoker.

…sallow hearts…

To the regions of the mystic north,
To the rocky shores of Whitby's sand
Where Stoker wrote his masterpiece,
Hidden in that haunted land.

Do you all not know
That every monster in embryo
Is borne from an ill played piano?
Its airs do spread like vampire wings
Over poorly protected, humble things.
And when the wild harbor glows at night
With an odious, translucent, ominous light
The colored panes of Saint Mary's show
Reds morose, upon the doomed archipelago
Warning us all of what exists down below.
And Stoker, drunk, over his morbid manuscript
Attempts to raise Lucifer's clan.
Saved or sullied, kept or ripped,
He hands the pages to the swallowing, tan
Dusk that has taken his psyche to the east,
To the Northern Sea, that boundless beast
Filled with hungry Sirens, all craving blood;
Their teeth, ivory as the Roman colonnades,
Their hearts, older than the freezing Celtic glades

IX

Fill Stoker's ink well with the all consuming flood
Of a despair far darker than of Dante's mind.
For literary fancy has become unkind -
And worse than real -
Which no desperate dawn can appease nor reveal

The slightest possibility of hope
As the author doth wail
He flees to the grasp of a tightly wound rope -
Dare you place your dear self in this horrible tale?

In *The Ghost Ship* Zwerenz pays tribute to Coleridge's
Ancient Mariner:.

*M*y vessel left Boston, seaward in the rain,
....I witnessed a commotion -
A vision reserved for the rabidly insane.

For above thick, nebulous billows,
Which clapped over the emerald sleep,
Like a shroud of gloomy, dreadful pillows,
Dark clouds did amass, foreboding and deep.

In the distance, barely seen on the watery court,
Sailed a cryptic schooner, wooden and old;
It swayed to either side in the maritime cold,
Wild and wavering from starboard to port.

And without rhyme or reason,
Devoid of any tangible treason,
This ship of ghastly vacancy
                                    X
Revealed to the eye not a soul on board.

And without a trace of clemency,
It leveled the waves like a terrible sword.
And then, to my abject horror I beheld

An animated corpse with skeletal hands
Clasping the wheel, on deck, alone,
Save for spiritual contrabands,
Which possessed that devilish specter's groan.

The horrid wraith did reel with the wind -
And an ominous rush, a poisoned zephyr,
Did cling to my neck, with the dusky scent
Of an ill and tainted tamarind,
A grave and dreadful, dark disease.
And then, with a hatred I had never known before,
His dead and steely eyes had bent
Over the infinite, oceanic floor
Before he exclaimed to me,
Through the black and dour, briny breeze,
Unhallowed, untamed on the ferocious sea:
"I am death,
And your hopeful desire
To reach the shore safely
Shall now expire
As I take you down -
To eternal fire!" ....

One poem Robert Louis Stevenson in Samoa 1894
XI

jarred my aesthetic equilibrium, because Robert
Louis Stevenson is the only writer I wish I had
known personally.

I shall go to the wine cellar
And retrieve some cold Chablis
In this dreadful chill of winter,
Encompassed within a dour ennui.

Outside on the frozen dales,
Aristocratic ladies daily change their faces
In eerie, haunted, dusky places
As the overwhelming daylight pales.

Yes, the tangerine sun -
It weeps and wails,
Delightful to no one;
Oh, these doleful, maddening tales! -

If I could only find the gate,
I would gladly assassinate
My ghastly imaginations,
Filled with innumerable specters of self hate;
And bitter recriminations.

Perhaps it is too late?
My dear, I am in the basement; Do come down here,

XII

And witness what I can not prevent.
Every slice of the decaying casement
Has left my breath without a vent -
And all has turned to a fatal malice.

And my face - Is it changed?
Is this the fate heaven has arranged?
O God, is there no solace
For the damned and the deranged!?

Lord Byron, once his favorite, evokes only horror
now:

I approached his mansion of dark gray stone.
…I inhaled his many deaths as I did dare to dream,
And then, I beheld a horrible sight:
For Lord Byron's ghost descended down the
stairway;
His countenance was white and I could hear him
say:
"You will not survive the coming night."

Then, from the graveyard, from each pale, sickly
reed,
I heard empty voices bereft of all hope
Rise from coffins, from the dreary slope
Which surrounded the house, as my brain did
bleed.
And Byron smiled as a maddened bard.
Then the moonlight bled through the ashen glass
XIII

And I fled to the foyer, into the black yard,
Mad beneath the rusty pass,
Hearing Byron laugh as the horrid night
Consumed the entirety of the accursed land.

And my own fate, doomed, passed from my soul
Forever unwhole,
Into the grip of his frozen hand. (from Byron's
Ghost)

The wandering is over for this Poet. He has come
home to "Patmos."

Living with Mary, in a rural place,
Saint John was but a diadem
In the golden crown of her royal grace.
And there each utterance was a sacred gem.
With unspeakable beauty she tended to the home.
And John, her faithful son, never thought to roam.
And on winter nights, beneath the stars,
She would kneel and pray, beside the glowing,
wooden bars.

And when they were forced to suffer a bitter
goodbye,
(For he was exiled in Patmos, an isolated isle.)
She still retained her lively faith and gorgeous
smile,
With a longing and a grievous sigh…

XIV

Then one evening, solemn and mild,
When the time for grieving had come to an end
For both mother and child,
He witnessed her rise

Above the dell where the reeds did bend.

With the moon at her feet,
Surrounded by twelve brilliant stars,
In the ineffable realm of celestial skies,
Her glorious Assumption was complete.
And so does end the sacred tale.
Ave Maria, gracia plena,
And holy Catholic heaven hail!
                    (Ode to St John)

I ventured out, one cold winter's night
To an isolated furrow, to a holly green pond.
I looked up high to the grand beyond,
And saw rumbling from the sky, a tremendous light.

No passers by did see me, no human eye did know
That I came to seek my Maker,
In the sun and on those trails of snow.

Still I heard no sound from Him.
Then I pleaded for a sign.
And I heard from God a distant voice:
"I am yours, and you are mine!"
                    XV

(Peace)

Byron wrote The days of our youth are the days of

our glory. John disagrees. Heaven is the lasting and real place for glory, and the Catholic Church, not Poetry is Heaven's muse. The desire for worldly fame is the whisper of a False Muse.

Do you all not know
That every monster in embryo
Is borne from an ill played piano?

The choice for him was the same as it was for The French novelist and art critic Charles Marie Huysmans, whose friend had observed, "There can only be one of two endings for such a writer, the gallows or the cross." John has chosen the latter.

Paul Franzetti   June 24, 2018

TO MARY

Tuus totus ego sum, et omnia mea tua sunt.

1

THE REGAL DAWN

On sumptuous evenings in late July,
I would scamper down diamond-studded
dunes,
Beneath an azure confusion of ethereal
moons.
And I slept in the sand where linnets fly.

I drank from a silver cup a cosmic brew.
I drowned in pelagic brines where cathedral
bells would ring.
In my rapture, I heard a chorus of seraphim
sing,
Wrapped in curtains of green, and petals of
dew.

And when I awoke to the ecstasy of the regal
dawn,
I witnessed the Deity resplendent and bright,
In command of all love, from morn until night
As I sat in astonishment, on a gold and holy,
emerald lawn.

ODE TO BRAM STOKER

Our sallow hearts, they crave true peace,
And so our carriage sallies forth
To the regions of the mystic north,
To the rocky shores of Whitby's sand
Where Stoker wrote his masterpiece,
Hidden in that haunted land.
Do you all not know
That every monster in embryo
Is borne from an ill played piano?
Its airs do spread like vampire wings
Over poorly protected, humble things.
And when the wild harbor glows at night
With an odious, translucent, ominous light
The colored panes of Saint Mary's show
Reds morose, upon the doomed archipelago
Warning us all of what exists down below.
And Stoker, drunk, over his morbid
manuscript
Attempts to raise Lucifer's clan.
Saved or sullied, kept or ripped,
He hands the pages to the swallowing, tan
Dusk that has taken his psyche to the east,
To the Northern Sea, that boundless beast
Filled with hungry Sirens, all craving blood;

Their teeth, ivory as the Roman colonnades,
Their hearts, older than the freezing Celtic
glades
Fill Stoker's ink well with the all consuming
flood
Of a despair far darker than of Dante's mind.
For literary fancy has become unkind -
And worse than real -
Which no desperate dawn can appease nor
reveal
The slightest possibility of hope
As the author doth wail
He flees to the grasp of a tightly wound rope -
Dare you place your dear self in this horrible
tale?

3

THE GARDEN

Your long, exquisite hair,
Resting upon your naked back,
Parted, straight, ineffable and fair,
Engraves upon my scarlet heart
Its ruby tinted rapture of black.

With a feminine decision,
All the tears I have shed forever depart
With one lover's acquisition.

For your unspoken sermon,
Solemn and true
Permeates the winter around me
Creating all anew.

Yes, now is the sacred hour,
Devoid of every haunting rue.
For all does bloom like a glimmering bower.
And your sable gaze and your perfumed
mane
Which I shall eternally ascertain
Exudes tones of a cello,
Hyacinths and the crimson rose,
In melodies which are soft and mellow,
In the still of a sunlit garden close.

4

DUSK

Wavering myrtles and mountainous boons
Rise to your palatial rooms
On a cliff, free from cares, in dusky hours,
Upon your marble squares, and radiant
bowers.

Curtains of purple which grace your chambers
Sway and part as autumnal perfumes
Waft in to touch your dwelling's members:

Your baby grands, your vases and blooms.

And every staircase you descend
In your dress of white, clad with lace,
Beams with the sun, as your pristine face
Reflects the pillars and the boughs which
bend.

Now is the time when the grand beyond
Flows in through the hush of stained glass
panes,
As tender as a symphony, rising from the wild
plains
When every scarlet hue and longing
correspond.

My dear beloved child, my sister of the
redolent breeze,
The night, umbrageous and blessed with
melodic accords
Has claimed your bastion, as its loyal and
loving lords
Summon your carriage,
As you pray upon your naked knees,
To take us to a sanctified marriage,
Among the bliss of the holy trees.

5

THE SONG OF JOHN KEATS

In the late, expansive breezes of the fall,
When humble poets seek to learn
Wisdom from the secrets of a Grecian urn
Streams of zephyrs through windows call.

What is that poignant melody
Which beckons the bard with its luminous art
Moving his all too sensitive heart
To the sunlit terrace, looking out to sea?

What are those lofty symphonies
Which tremble through his iridescent rooms
Emitting an air which, scented, blooms
Like the rose from his ink well's rhapsodies?

6

THE GROVE

The sandy grove dressed with cherry trees
Wears carmines and other hues, delicate and
yellow.
It stands among a stream, azure, soft and

mellow
Which glimmers in the sun, caressed by the
breeze.

I arrived from the Floridian Keys
On a vessel in three weeks time,
Landing on the coast of France,
Weaving mystic rhyme,
In a sailor's pining, romantic trance,
In search of regal pleasantries.

I happened upon a rustic, old inn
Where I heard the strains of a violin.
And, behold, I met a lady fair,
And the scent of blossoms in her raven hair.

She brought me a glass of Belgian beer
And sat down with a feminine charm, beside
me;
And my eyes, they shed a sacred tear,
For I knew she was my bride to be.

Then we walked onto an emerald dale,
Where the purple sun set beyond the farms.
With tender kisses and open arms,
We loved one another as the day did pale.

And as the moon rose high
Into the canvass of the night,
We found ourselves immersed in light,

And met the eve with a grateful sigh.

7

THE GHOST SHIP

My vessel left Boston, seaward in the rain,
As I ferried to the east, to the vast, Italian
main.
Half way across the ocean,
In a tempest, my emotion
Turned from tranquility to disdain
As I witnessed a commotion -
A vision reserved for the rabidly insane.

For above thick, nebulous billows,
Which clapped over the emerald sleep,
Like a shroud of gloomy, dreadful pillows,
Dark clouds did amass, foreboding and deep.

In the distance, barely seen on the watery
court,
Sailed a cryptic schooner, wooden and old;
It swayed to either side in the maritime cold,
Wild and wavering from starboard to port.

And without rhyme or reason,
Devoid of any tangible treason,
This ship of ghastly vacancy
Revealed to the eye not a soul on board.

And without a trace of clemency,
It leveled the waves like a terrible sword.
And then, to my abject horror I beheld
An animated corpse with skeletal hands
Clasping the wheel, on deck, alone,
Save for spiritual contrabands,
Which possessed that devilish specter's
groan.

The horrid wraith did reel with the wind -
And an ominous rush, a poisoned zephyr,
Did cling to my neck, with the dusky scent
Of an ill and tainted tamarind,
A grave and dreadful, dark disease.
And then, with a hatred I had never known
before,
His dead and steely eyes had bent
Over the infinite, oceanic floor
Before he exclaimed to me,
Through the black and dour, briny breeze,
Unhallowed, untamed on the ferocious sea:
"I am death,
And your hopeful desire
To reach the shore safely
Shall now expire
As I take you down -
To eternal fire!"

8

DIADEMS

I fashioned the wings of my spirit
With the ethereal tears of black, spotted
butterflies,
Intoxicated with the noonday sun.

I greeted the most egregious heresies
Committed by austere tyrants,
And, using spiritual alchemy,
By mercy, transformed those savage
apostates
Into pious servants, one by one.

I wandered beneath the brine kissed stars;
Endless trails of grass
In mystic woodlands
Opened like ecstatic dahlias;
Each one promised eternal happiness
By appearing as moonlit, mysterious sands,
Clad with wondrous forms of reedy hopes.

I took all dawns as miracles;
On summer nights, on fire,
I resurrected chivalry
From the pages of my poems,

Writ in streams with leaves for a pen,
Every line dedicated to the servants of The
Virgin.

I warned the black knights
In their mad, metallic arrogance
To beware of Dante's circular hells:
Nine in number, never knowing an end.

Forsaking sleep, I conversed with angels.
All romances became waterfalls.
And my bride descended like a paradisal
queen
From the heights of Jerusalem, adorned with
diadems,
Of regal purples, jades and gems.

9

THE LANE

We walked as angels in the rosy breeze,
Among holly green hedgerows (just us two).
The lane was gold and the sky was blue,
And we heard through the boughs rare
symphonies,
As the grasses framed your naked knees.

Descending from the leafy branches, each

note borne from above,
Graced our enraptured hearts, flowing like a
joyful stream,
As we lost ourselves in a wondrous dream,
Finally finding the meaning of
The rising moon which crowned our love!

10

THE SHRINE OF SAINT ANNE

After the rain had fallen on the town,
Beyond the maze of city streets,
Where sounds become suburban retreats
I found a shrine upon a down.

Silhouettes of oaks, and an iron fence
Found me amid blooms which marked the
entrance.
With dappled rays, the sun did set
Over my trail, as I crossed a rivulet.

Slender fountains and marble floors of white
Bathing in the umbrage of the wavering trees
Emitted a concerto in the redolent breeze.

And in one corner of the shrine's pure light
I beheld the spirit of good Saint Anne,
And discovered what it means to be a holy

man.

11

THE WINDOW BAY

The window, half open, beyond the bay, looks
out to sea,
While a black baby grand plays in a minor key
A melancholic air,
Enamored with rhyme.

It speaks of a former life,
A solemn ardor, banished by time,
Calling to mind the eyes of my wife.

And every time I hear it played,
My heart becomes younger, and less afraid
In the broad, yellow sun,
Streaming from the cosmic sea,
Over the grottos, where linnets sound their
summery voice,
And once again, our hearts are one,
Forever to rejoice -
Triumphantly!

12

STILLED BY A SIGH

Her vein is tranquil, and more than fair.
Her speech is terse, yet debonair.
Her braided tresses are long and black,
And rest like gems upon her back.

Her gaze, it gleams like jewels in the shade,
On the arboreal scented misty shore.
Her kisses are of cinnamon, and as I pine for
more,
We hear the happy din, from beyond the
promenade.

Atop the mounts, the stars duly rise, with
Venus on high.
Along with the moon, they bestow their light
To soft siroccos; and as they sanctify the
coming night,
All music is stilled - by the song of our sigh.

13

HER SILKEN KISS

I wandered through the country side at night,
In search of a virtuous, pious bride.
On a rustic lane, with hyacinths on either side,
I beheld a raven mane, gleaming in the
moonlight.
Each tress was long and straight, her eyes
were dark;
She appeared as an angel, in that solemn
park,
And her voice was one of a statue's stone -
Pure and profound, of an exalted tone.
She took my hand in a garden close,
Where the scent of lilacs, emitted from her
lips,
Sent my psyche into rapture, as my silken
heart took sips
From her soft, silken buss borne of sunshine
and the rose.

14

THE HALF OPENED WINDOW

How many days in the year
I must live without you?
My bride, my love, my only, my dear.
The gold, summer sun shines above and
about you,
And in the redolent, solemn breeze I hear
Over the somnolent ponds of blue
The effete, acrostic rhythms which flow
From the iridescent, luminous bower
Through the half opened window
Hymns of a resolute, relentless flow
Which permeate the hallowed hour.

They haunt me so, those melancholic airs
Sacrosanct, allotropic, like a mysterious sun
Filled with the lethargy of a dim despair,
As they enter my chamber, with imprecision,
Calling my soul, morose yet immortal,
To poignant thoughts of days gone by.

And the minutes pace, and the hours weep
Like sands in a glass, as I resolutely keep
Your angelic face within my mind
Born from the gardens that wistfully sleep
In an atmosphere untouched, unkind.

15

AFTER MANY SULLEN YEARS

After many sullen years
Of numb confusion and abject pain
I have become inconstant as a weathervane.
And my bitter tears
Trailing from blind eyes
Which sees evil and good
With an identical gaze
Gives rise to hollow, remorseless cries
In the forsaken wood, as my wayward ways
Ascend to empty, clueless skies.
And my faith does pale
With each passing morn,
As I go hither and there, wanton and worn. -
O, the sad and tragic tale!

16

ISOLATION

The iridescent sky
At the peak of its beauty
Reigns like a cosmic oligarchy
Knowing every when, where and why.

And the reedy trail, bathed in sunlight
Which I travel upon, as a vagabond,
Beckons me to contemplate the great beyond
Where infinite peace is married to delight.

There are pianos playing in the trees by the
piers
On either side of the breeze blown lane.
There are mystic wines within the rain,
Which sanctify my pages, wet - as with tears.

17

ONE FINE DAY
One fine, golden day,
Donning a pea coat, happily,
Trodding through majestic garden closes,
I wandered freely as one can be,
Amid mellow daisies, and scarlet roses.

I passed by a wooden trellis of white,
Strewn with ivory, and struck by the sunlight,
On my way to the regal, vast village square,
To a royal wedding by the sea,
Where a young, handsome man and his
maiden fair

Enraptured with ecstasy, in the amorous air,
Pledged eternal vows of fidelity.

And they walked as a true king and queen
For one glorious day.
And from balconies above,
Made from stone and clad with florets of
green,
Palms of victory did joyfully sway
To celebrate their love,
In the quaint, little town, by the blue, rustic
bay.

18

ROBERT LOUIS STEVENSON
SAMOA, 1894

I shall go to the wine cellar
And retrieve some cold chablis
In this dreadful chill of winter,
Encompassed within a dour ennui.

Outside on the frozen dales,
Aristocratic ladies daily change their faces
In eerie, haunted, dusky places
As the overwhelming daylight pales.

Yes, the tangerine sun -
It weeps and wails,
Delightful to no one;
Oh, these doleful, maddening tales! -

If I could only find the gate,
I would gladly assassinate
My ghastly imaginations,
Filled with innumerable specters of self hate;
And bitter recriminations.

Perhaps it is too late?
My dear, I am in the basement; Do come
down here,
And witness what I can not prevent.
Every slice of the decaying casement
Has left my breath without a vent -
And all has turned to a fatal malice.
And my face - Is it changed?
Is this the fate heaven has arranged?
O God, is there no solace
For the damned and the deranged!?

19

BYRON'S GHOST

In the furrows of Byron, I roved alone,

Though a throng of oaks and shady willows.
Beneath a firmament of ivory billows,
I approached his mansion of dark gray stone.

I inhaled his many deaths as I did dare to
dream,
Passing through an ominous silhouette I went,
Beneath an ancient ogive, where its boughs
were long and bent,
Where a rusty iron gate hovered over a
cloudy stream.

The foyer was tuneless, and the panes were
dark.
In the hall no life existed save spiritual
contraband,
A solitary candle was lit by a hand
Unseen to the eyes. Outside, in the park
I imagined I glimpsed a phantom of hate.
The boughs, by harsh gales seemed to relate
Perdition as they crashed together.
The sky grew dim, and I wondered whether
I should leave the realm of that haunted
estate.

And then, I beheld a horrible sight:
For Lord Byron's ghost descended down the
stairway;
His countenance was white and I could hear
him say:

"You will not survive the coming night."

Then, from the graveyard, from each pale,
sickly reed,
I heard empty voices bereft of all hope
Rise from coffins, from the dreary slope
Which surrounded the house, as my brain did
bleed.
And Byron smiled as a maddened bard.
Then the moonlight bled through the ashen
glass
And I fled to the foyer, into the black yard,
Mad beneath the rusty pass,
Hearing Byron laugh as the horrid night
Consumed the entirety of the accursed land.
And my own fate, doomed, passed from my
soul
Forever unwhole,
Into the grip of his frozen hand.

20

SAINT JOHN'S WOOD

When brown guitars ring softly down
The cobblestone streets
Where every vine of each lattice meets,
I hear sobbing in the skies which grace the
town.

In long, cryptic shadows, in the redolent
shade,
Hidden beneath the red disguise of dying
leaves,
With their bended heads wavering in the
baleful breeze,
Far off, solemn vows are reluctantly made.

Singing in a minor key,
Two lovers walk in the suburban rains
Where an obscure beauty gleams on the
lanes
Completing their dreams tenuously.

Uncertain of their nuptial designs,
To and fro, they wander as warm gales
Glide through their hair as daylight pales
Over the silent houses, serenading their
minds.

And then the moon, in its profound luminosity,
Reveals each to the other's admiring eyes
Their nebulous doubt - which lives and dies.

The approaching dawn harkens beyond what
they can see:
Holding a future concealed behind a veil,
Whispering each to the other an untold tale.

21

SAINT PAUL'S CATHEDRAL

In the shadows of Saint Paul's Cathedral,
Beneath the gray stones of its ancient wall,
I embraced your hair and its braided bows.
Its raven tresses outshined the stars,
And thrilled my soul from head to toe.
And all my years of unyielding woe
Are changed to airs borne of white guitars.
And then I hear you speak my name,
With a softness no poet could ever pen.
As we walked into your warm, cozy den,
With a gentle hush the moonlight came,
And it rests upon your sable mane.

Now a symphony of violins
Fall into your gaze like an angel's wings,
Into the deep dark browns of your immaculate
eyes,
Which speak to me of mandolins.
And all the pure and humble things
Which grace your chamber, along with my
love,
Are lit from above,
As a saint complies

With the very hues of heaven
Which live within your eyes.

22

SAILING

I set off for London from the coast of
Normandy,
In an old, wooden schooner,
Laden with gold.
The billows were cold and briny.
And the rising evening fell much sooner -
Much sooner than I had been told.
The stars were drunk with cosmic wine,
And the firmament was boundless and bright.
I was immersed in a canopy of mystic light,
In zephyrs of bluish brine -
Which endowed the deck
With the scents of night!

23

ODE TO SAINT JOHN

Living with Mary, in a rural place,
Saint John was but a diadem
In the golden crown of her royal grace.

And there each utterance was a sacred gem.

With unspeakable beauty she tended to the
home.
And John, her faithful son, never thought to
roam.
And on winter nights, beneath the stars,
She would kneel and pray, beside the
glowing, wooden bars.

And when they were forced to suffer a bitter
goodbye,
(For he was exiled in Patmos, an isolated
isle.)
She still retained her lively faith and gorgeous
smile,
With a longing and a grievous sigh.

And upon his return
Her heart did burn
To see her Son in Paradise,
And the glory of God, Holy Thrice.
How his tender heart did purely burn!

Then one evening, solemn and mild,
When the time for grieving had come to an
end
For both mother and child,
He witnessed her rise
Above the dell where the reeds did bend.

With the moon at her feet,
Surrounded by twelve brilliant stars,
In the ineffable realm of celestial skies,
Her glorious Assumption was complete.
And so does end the sacred tale.
Ave Maria, gracia plena,
And holy Catholic heaven hail!

24

THE FARMHOUSE

I arrived in a Portuguese port at dawn,
And wandered to a rustic inn.
I sat in a booth amid the lively din;
A chandelier above me lit my view of the
lawn,
The meadow beyond, of dew and grain.
I ordered an ale from a pretty waitress,
With dark, black ringlets in her hair.
We walked to a farmhouse in the summer
rain,
And I loved her until noon - resting on her

dress.
The fragrance of her dew clad breast laced the aromatic air
With scents of thyme and mignonette.
We found peace in the hay-
A lovely coquette,
She haunts my psyche to this day.
Then we roved through a garden, a florid square,
Where terra cotta statues stood beside the vines
Sprawling heavenward to fantastic columns, gleaming in the light.
And we fell into one another's visual wines,
Devoted to hearts of tender fire, and kisses of the night.

25

THE STORM

I awoke to a storm in an ancient time.
The rain fell upon the branches and the vines,
And filled the streams of eglantines,
As in my notes I penned metered rhyme.

The moon up high did weep with a tear,
Next to the lane, in a silhouette of the silent wood.

Willows and roses wavered where I stood,
As the fragrant breeze tasted of mystic beer.

And in the hour when the sun went down,
Over the plains of a distant brown,
I beheld a lass, more beautiful than life.

She smiled as an angel, and took me by my
hand,
Sighing like a siren, upon the grassy land,
And I knew from her kiss she would be my
wife.

26

CHILLINGHAM CASTLE

Hungry from my excursions, and thirsty from
the sun,
I came upon an immense estate,
Nestled far from this weary world of strife.
Indeed, it seemed severed from life,
And it looked as though I was the only one
To find this place, but alas too late -
For I saw not a soul to aid my condition.

The entrance was imposing to sight and to
sound,

For the loneliness of such a cold, dark place
Made my dizzy head spin round and round.
I beheld no forms, no voices, no face,
Which resembled a human over the entire
ground.

I made my way to the keep of the mansion.
Where I made a discovery, dim and dour.
For a grave with an inscription there,
In the horror of that bastion,
In the terror of the stifling air,
Indeed, spelled my name - as I passed
through a veil -
With a pitiful and desperate, helpless wail -
In the dire blackness of my final hour.

27

BLOSSOMS IN HER HAIR

How lovely her grace seems to me,
When she wanders through the courtyard
In a state of precious grace.
There angels praise the symphony of her
ineffable face,
As she walks near the undulating sea,
Where the briny wind speaks of her masculine
bard.

How delicate are her braided bows,

Where a stream from paradise gently flows,
Crowning her a queen, as she kneels in the
square;
For from sanctity she will never part,
With ardor in her sacred heart,
And cherry blossoms in her hair.

28

ROSES ON THE WAVES

On my way to meet you,
I gathered and brought a new bouquet,
Of the earth's finest florets,
From a gilded dale of gleaming hay.
And knowing you lived upon an isle,
I had to swim from my boat to shore,
And while I swam to you,
I lost every rose in the sounding sea,
In the violence of a downward pour.
And so each bloom was graced with brine,
Like a dappled poem of mystic wine.

Now that I have recovered from the billows of
the sea,
Where the waves were strewn with petals,
Beneath the firmament of azure blue.
Falling in circles, in the summery sun,
Please accept these redolent souvenirs from

me,
And the scarlet fragrances they bestow on
you,
As they unite our perfumed love as true,
Your face as an angel's, our heart as one.

29

MY LOVE

My love can not be found in the verse of Poe.
Nor in Shakespeare's litanies of the wise
man's woe.
Verily, I tell you, you will not find her there,
Resting upon a balcony, in a state of
swooning, mad despair.

For no Romeo can lure her from my arms.
(She yields her secret charms
To me and to my heart alone.)
The sunlight beams on her bastion made of
stone,
Where she walks to her royal carriage,
Dreaming of a sacred marriage,
And a knight (none but I) she can truly call her
own.

30

A SANCTIFIED FLAME

I must have lived a long time ago,
When your long, black hair met the contrast of
the snow.
And your smile of an angel's filled my heart
with a sacred flame.
Into my life, as a blessing, you came,
As a mystic, sunlit sirocco.
And my psyche and heart have never been
the same
Ever since I beheld your holy sight.
For the cadence of your flowing name
Renders dead the rues of all my plight.

31

ON SOFT, SPRING NIGHTS

On soft spring nights,
When the sun is in the west,
Dying over the saffron crest
Of the purple, jagged mount,
On the passing clouds I count
The blissful boons of the April lights
When my every kiss can love you best.

And when my eyes do run their sacred trail
From your raven tresses to your silver feet,
There begins the holy, chivalric tale
Which makes whole our ardor, triumphant,
complete.

32

IN SHADOWS ON FOOT

In shadows on foot, I strolled alone.
In search of true love and an inn for rest.
I drank mystic liquors, on my knees,
In a wondrous grove of apple trees,
And I declared you as my solemn queen
Whom I would serve, whom I loved best.
For on the banks of a wide, lush ravine,
Where a rivulet splashed over stone,
I saw you picking rare, bright flowers,
Hyacinths and lilacs, yellow daffodils,
With joyful tears, in the scented shadows of
dusky hours,
In aromatic dells, on brilliant, mystic hills.

33

PEACE

I ventured out, one cold winter's night
To an isolated furrow, to a holly green pond.
I looked up high to the grand beyond,
And saw rumbling from the sky a tremendous
light.

No passersby did see me, no human eye did
know
That I came to seek my Maker,
In the sun and on those trails of snow.

Still I heard no sound from Him.
Then I pleaded for a sign.
And I heard from God a distant voice:
"I am yours, and you are mine!"

34

SHE WALKS BEYOND

She walks beyond the vine-clad stone, In the
English shade, to a garden of sun. Her spirit
and her flesh are one; She walks in peace, to

the glade, alone.

There are ebonies which call her To epiphanies of yellow light. And when the scented breeze Through the linden trees stir She reveals herself as royalty In the diamond glow of heaven's sight.

And then, Next to a bench of marble in the garden, Where statues stand, clad with eglantines, A fountain rises to the cloudless sky Rejoicing in her beauty, With a silver sigh As her dark eyes gaze upon the sunny vines.

And all the earth is a symphony As every star sobs with majesty, Fair and solemn, sacred and of glory; She walks upon the promenade, Pondering rapture, and ecstasy In the melodious bower of the sanctified glade. Her thoughts are of felicity, As the lavender sunset touches every rose, With a summery grace, Bestowing gold upon her face, Where she walks in the little garden-close.

35

TEARS

Another dawn,
I am alone, forlorn.
One priest did say
I will never see her
In a lovely way
When in heaven we shall forever live.

Beyond all years,
Beyond all strife,
The one, sole comfort I have had in this life
Is having shed so many tears.

36

THE COURTYARD

I will tell you truly with my heart
Just how lovely you are, my dear.
The rain clouds fade,
And slowly depart
Under the gold of the sun's chandelier.

That descending gilded orb, over every

ancient rampart,
In the courtyard where you wade,
On the marble's silhouettes, of their every
colonnade,
Praises with grace your angelic face in
heaven's sight.

Near fountains which sob, rising slender in the
shade,
You touch every star, in the firmament of
moonlight.
Your regal countenance, looking out to sea,
Overwhelms my psyche,
Which transfers to my soul
Things which words can not express.

For you make my spirit whole,
As you dream among the statuary, holy in that
sacred place,
Donning a bright and splendid dress,
Clad with frills and long, white lace.

37

THE DRIEST PLACE

Yes, there are many tears to cry.
In our collective orphanage,
In our common well

That has run dry, verily as the driest place.
Wherefore art is our love and our duty to our
Thrice good Sage?
And of our destiny, who can tell,
Whence comes death in the final hour?

Tell me, then,
Will you attain that gold, bright garden,
That holy and heavenly, infinite bower?
Or will you find it horrid and odd
To have your soul
Swallowed whole
In the ominous fate of Marquis De Sade?

And when you die,
Will you leave in grace?

Yes, there are many tears to cry.
And yes, this world is the driest place.

38

THE GOOD ROAD'S END

I wandered beyond many thankless hills to a
barren wood,
Beneath frozen firmaments; and as often as I
could,
I would warm myself in the boons of a
hearth's gold flames,

Encompassed by many leafless trees, yet
each devoid of names.

A silhouetted reticence reigned in the night.
Every sanguine bough was shaken by the
merciless cold.
Gales rended branches like thieves at twilight,
And I heard in their echos a sapience for the
old.

My worn, brittle boots breached the
untouched pall
Of the vast, virginal meadow, as sheets of
snow began to fall.
Every flake spoke of reason, coupled with
grace.

Their silent epiphanies clothed the umbrage
of the mead,
As they covered the hidden browns of every
chestnut reed: -
One often finds God in a lonely place.

THE ASCENSION

I

HADES

I began the long journey with one weary
advance,
As a homeless villager, quite alone in the
world.
As subterraneous pits unfurled,
I opened my psyche to the endless, dreadful
dance.

There were demons on fire with a lust for
unkindness
As they turned from truth and indulged in
blindness,
Turning the damned over coals in fire,
In Satan's black chapel where he rules in
pain.

His entire existence is one lived in vain.
For he chose to murder, his only desire
Ever since his inception, envying man:
Fashioned in God's likeness, born for God's
kind,
Destined for a celestial body, to be another

god.

The devil could not suffer this, and so the rebellion began.
"I will prevail!" he swore, in his witless, infant mind.
And though it might seem obscure and odd,
Nothing but fire did the demon find.

Afraid of all below and above,
He prowls and travels as an arsonist on leave.
{So he thinks.}
And the only moments he can bare is when he drinks
Vodkas, rums, and biles from the slums,
He knows naught of how to love,
He knows naught of how to grieve.
{To hatred alone he utterly succumbs.}

II

THE COUNTRYSIDE

And as I raised a toast in the knell
Of a rustic and old, quaint French inn,
I decided I had enough of hell.
So I danced with a waitress, in that blessed place,
To the happy chime of a distant church bell;
So we took a covered carriage to the festivals

and the squares,
And our romance did begin.
{She wore an ivory dress, made of the finest
lace.}
I left her more than mirthful, placing roses on
classical airs,
On an old and russet mandolin.

III

THE END

Then as the dawn crept over the greenery,
I awoke to my notebook for the very last time.
And I took in the hills, the canvass and its
scenery,
Seeking, like a beggar, a nickel or a dime.

40

MY GOD, THRICE HOLY

Holy Trinity

Help my poor soul,
And never abandon me
To myself;
For no one but Thee
Can render my spirit whole.
In the consecrated furnace,
Before the witness of the angelic host -
Here upon the earth.

Spare me from purification
After death,
And do, by Thy Kingly might
Welcome my being Into the radiant sight
Of your thrice victorious face,
In this life and in eternity -
Of charity, peace, and ineffable grace.

In nomine Patris et Filii et Spiritus Sancti

AMEN

Published by ATLApublishing.com

Made in the USA
Middletown, DE
14 November 2022

14978868R00046